Made in the USA
Monee, IL
27 March 2022

93625666R10069